D1756837

Comhairle Contae
Átha Cliath Theas
South Dublin County Council

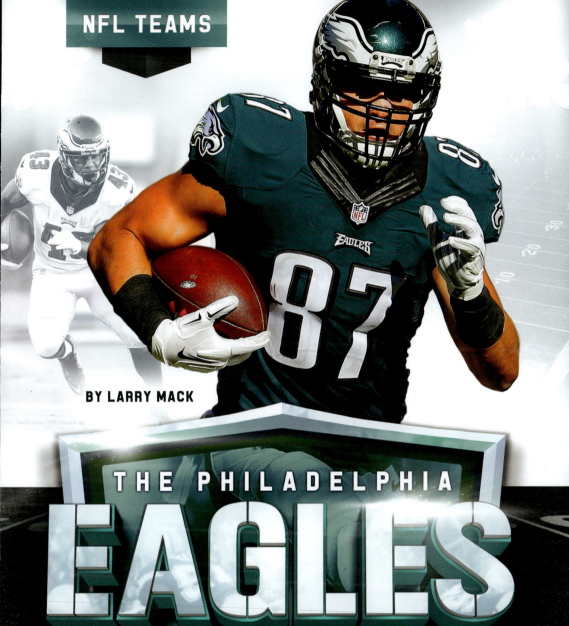

BY LARRY MACK

THE PHILADELPHIA
EAGLES
STORY

BELLWETHER MEDIA · MINNEAPOLIS, MN

TM

Are you ready to take it to the extreme? Torque books thrust you into the action-packed world of sports, vehicles, mystery, and adventure. These books may include dirt, smoke, fire, and chilling tales. **WARNING**: read at your own risk.

This edition first published in 2017 by Bellwether Media, Inc.

No part of this publication may be reproduced in whole or in part without written permission of the publisher. For information regarding permission, write to Bellwether Media, Inc., Attention: Permissions Department, 5357 Penn Avenue South, Minneapolis, MN 55419.

Library of Congress Cataloging-in-Publication Data

Names: Mack, Larry, author.
Title: The Philadelphia Eagles Story / by Larry Mack.
Description: Minneapolis, MN : Bellwether Media, Inc., 2017. | Series:
   Torque: NFL Teams | Includes bibliographical references and index.
Identifiers: LCCN 2015046404 | ISBN 9781626173781 (hardcover : alk. paper)
Subjects: LCSH: Philadelphia Eagles (Football team)–History–Juvenile literature.
Classification: LCC GV956.P44 M33 2017 | DDC 796.332/640974811–dc23
LC record available at http://lccn.loc.gov/2015046404

Text copyright © 2017 by Bellwether Media, Inc. TORQUE and associated logos are trademarks and/or registered trademarks of Bellwether Media, Inc.

SCHOLASTIC, CHILDREN'S PRESS, and associated logos are trademarks and/or registered trademarks of Scholastic Inc.

Printed in the United States of America, North Mankato, MN.

TABLE OF CONTENTS

The Philadelphia Eagles face the Dallas Cowboys on December 29, 2013. The winner heads to the National Football League (NFL) **playoffs**. The loser's season ends.

Nick Foles

Brent Celek

The Eagles are ahead in the second quarter. Eagles **tight end** Brent Celek catches a pass from **quarterback** Nick Foles. He sprints for a touchdown! The Eagles lead 17 to 10 at halftime.

Bryce Brown

The Cowboys almost catch up in the third quarter. But the Eagles keep rolling. They score another touchdown in the fourth quarter.

Then, with minutes remaining, the Cowboys score a touchdown. They try for a two-point conversion to tie the game. But a diving Eagle defender knocks the ball from the Cowboys! The Eagles hold on to win!

NO LOVE LOST

The Eagles and Cowboys are two of football's most bitter rivals. Since 1960, the teams have battled more than 100 times.

SCORING TERMS

END ZONE
the area at each end of a football field; a team scores by entering the opponent's end zone with the football.

EXTRA POINT
a score that occurs when a kicker kicks the ball between the opponent's goal posts after a touchdown is scored; 1 point.

FIELD GOAL
a score that occurs when a kicker kicks the ball between the opponent's goal posts; 3 points.

SAFETY
a score that occurs when a player on offense is tackled behind his own goal line; 2 points for defense.

TOUCHDOWN
a score that occurs when a team crosses into its opponent's end zone with the football; 6 points.

TWO-POINT CONVERSION
a score that occurs when a team crosses into its opponent's end zone with the football after scoring a touchdown; 2 points.

The Eagles are known for some of the NFL's most loyal fans. After each touchdown, the team's fight song blasts over the stadium speakers. Fans loudly sing along. Some flap their arms like wings!

In the 2000s, fans rooted for the Eagles in five National Football **Conference** (NFC) Championship games. They also cheered them all the way to **Super Bowl** 39!

LINCOLN FINANCIAL FIELD

The Eagles play their home games at Lincoln Financial Field in Philadelphia, Pennsylvania. Fans call this stadium "The Linc."

The Linc has many energy-saving features. It is one of the "greenest" stadiums in the world. **Solar panels** supply much of its electricity. **Wind turbines** also power the stadium.

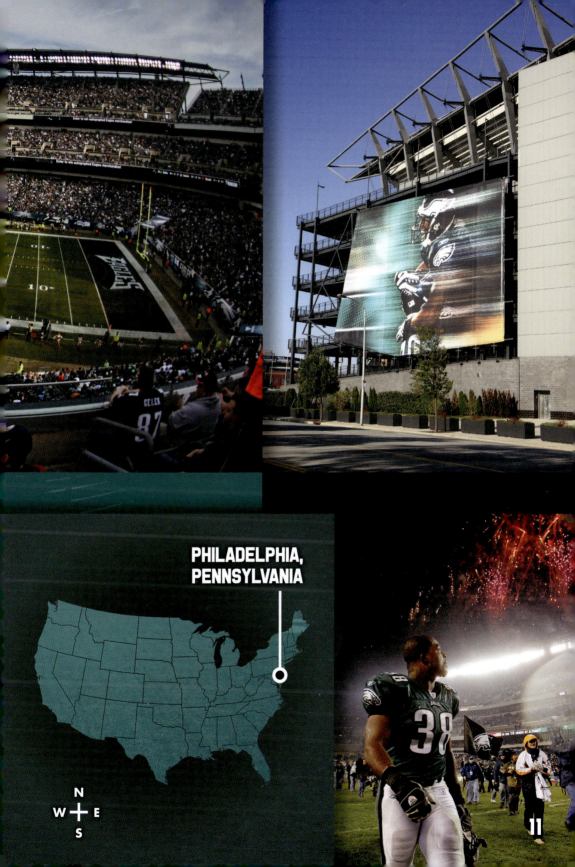

PHILADELPHIA, PENNSYLVANIA

N
W E
S

The Eagles play in the NFC East **Division**. The other three NFC East teams are the Eagles' fierce **rivals**. The New York Giants are the oldest rival. The Dallas Cowboys and Washington Redskins are the Eagles' other division opponents.

NFL DIVISIONS

 **AFC**

AFC NORTH

 BALTIMORE **RAVENS**

 CINCINNATI **BENGALS**

 CLEVELAND **BROWNS**

 PITTSBURGH **STEELERS**

AFC EAST

 BUFFALO **BILLS**

 MIAMI **DOLPHINS**

 NEW ENGLAND **PATRIOTS**

 NEW YORK **JETS**

AFC SOUTH

 HOUSTON **TEXANS**

 INDIANAPOLIS **COLTS**

 JACKSONVILLE **JAGUARS**

 TENNESSEE **TITANS**

AFC WEST

 DENVER **BRONCOS**

 KANSAS CITY **CHIEFS**

 OAKLAND **RAIDERS**

 SAN DIEGO **CHARGERS**

NFC NORTH

 CHICAGO
BEARS

 DETROIT
LIONS

 GREEN BAY
PACKERS

MINNESOTA
VIKINGS

NFC EAST

 DALLAS
COWBOYS

 NEW YORK
GIANTS

 PHILADELPHIA
EAGLES

 WASHINGTON
REDSKINS

NFC SOUTH

 ATLANTA
FALCONS

 CAROLINA
PANTHERS

 NEW ORLEANS
SAINTS

TAMPA BAY
BUCCANEERS

NFC WEST

 ARIZONA
CARDINALS

 LOS ANGELES
RAMS

 SAN FRANCISCO
49ERS

  SEATTLE
SEAHAWKS

The Eagles' first season was 1933. That year, Bert Bell and Lud Wray bought a local team called the Yellow Jackets. The team name changed to the Eagles.

In 1941, Alexis Thompson became owner and Earle "Greasy" Neale became head coach. Neale shaped the Eagles into a top team. They won NFL titles with him in 1948 and 1949.

Bert Bell

Earle Neale

JOINING FORCES

Many teams did not have enough players during World War II. The Eagles and Pittsburgh Steelers combined teams to make the "Steagles" in 1943!

The 1960s and 1970s were tough years. But in 1981, head coach Dick Vermeil led the Eagles to Super Bowl 15. The team reached the Super Bowl again in 2005 with head coach Andy Reid.

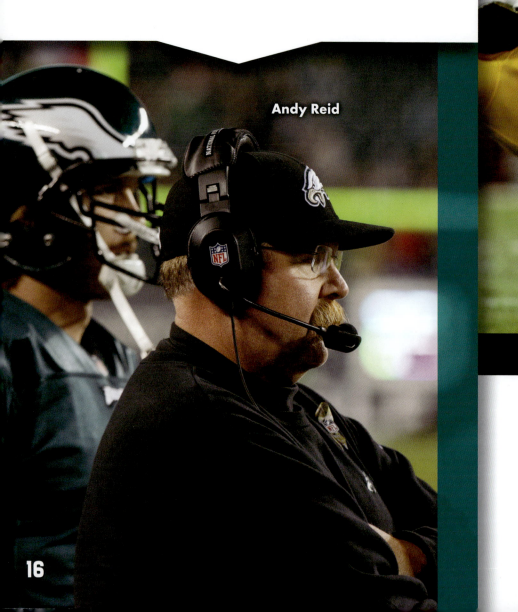

Andy Reid

Darren Sproles

Today, the team has talented players like **running back** Darren Sproles. These players hope to bring the city a Super Bowl win!

TIMELINE

1933

Played their first NFL game

1943

Joined the Steelers for one season to form the "Steagles"

1948

Won their first NFL title, beating the Chicago Cardinals (7-0)

1939

Played the Brooklyn Dodgers in the first televised pro football game

1949

Defended their NFL title, beating the Los Angeles Rams (14-0)

1981

Played in Super Bowl 15, but lost to the Oakland Raiders

10   FINAL SCORE   **27**

2005

Played in Super Bowl 39, but lost to the New England Patriots

21   FINAL SCORE   **24**

1960

Won the team's third NFL Championship, beating the Green Bay Packers (17-13)

1984

Drafted Hall-of-Fame defensive end Reggie White

2009

Played in their fifth NFC Championship game of the decade

Many great Eagles have played quarterback. Ron Jaworski led the Eagles to Super Bowl 15. Donovan McNabb brought the team to Super Bowl 39.

Donovan McNabb

WELCOME TO THE NFL

In 1935, Eagles owner Bert Bell suggested the first NFL draft. This gave all teams an equal chance to choose talented college players.

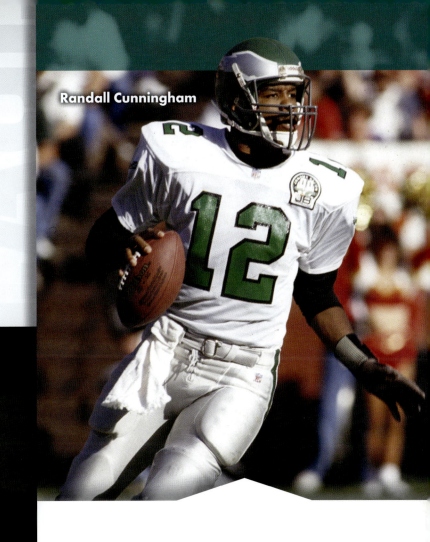

Randall Cunningham

NFL coaches and staff twice voted Eagles quarterback Randall Cunningham player of the year. Sometimes Cunningham also played **punter**. In one game, he punted the ball 91 yards!

The Eagles have also had great defenders. One early star was Chuck Bednarik. The **linebacker** played 14 seasons with the Eagles.

Defensive end Reggie White **sacked** opposing quarterbacks 124 times in 121 games. **Safety** Brian Dawkins made 34 **interceptions** for the Eagles.

TEAM GREATS

CHUCK BEDNARIK
LINEBACKER

RON JAWORSKI
QUARTERBACK

REGGIE WHITE
DEFENSIVE END

Brian Dawkins

SICK DEFENSE

The 1991 Eagles defense was one of the NFL's best ever. They earned the nickname "Gang Green." It is a play on "gangrene," a dangerous medical condition.

RANDALL CUNNINGHAM
QUARTERBACK
1985–1995

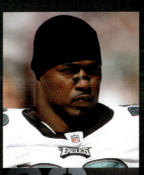

BRIAN DAWKINS
SAFETY
1996–2008

DONOVAN McNABB
QUARTERBACK
1999–2009

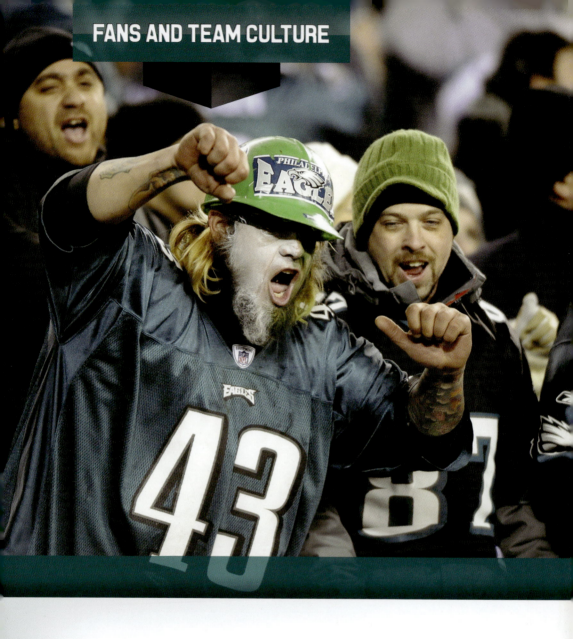

Loyal Eagles fans joke that they bleed green, the team's color. They are some of the NFL's loudest fans. Along with their fight song, they are known to make fun of opponents.

Eagles fans also show their loyalty in other ways. In 2014, they bought 5,000 playoff tickets in 10 minutes!

DREAM COME TRUE

In 1976, schoolteacher and Philadelphia Eagles fan Vince Papale became an Eagle! The movie *Invincible* tells his story.

Eagles fans hope their faith will bring their city a Super Bowl title. The Eagles know their fans expect it. The team has come close a number of times. But no matter what happens, fans look forward to a new season every fall!

Swoop

MORE ABOUT THE EAGLES

Team name:
Philadelphia Eagles

Team name explained:
**Inspired by an eagle
symbol used by the United
States government**

Nicknames:
The Birds, Gang Green

Joined NFL: 1933

Conference: NFC

Division: East

**Main rivals: New York Giants,
Dallas Cowboys**

Hometown:
Philadelphia, Pennsylvania

Training camp location:
**NovaCare Complex,
Philadelphia, Pennsylvania**

PENNSYLVANIA

N
W + E
S

PHILADELPHIA

Home stadium name:
Lincoln Financial Field

Stadium opened: 2003

Seats in stadium: 69,176

Logo: **A white and
silver eagle head facing
left, outlined in black
and green**

Colors: **Midnight green,
silver, black, white**

Mascot: Swoop

GLOSSARY

conference—a large grouping of sports teams that often play one another

defensive end—a player on defense whose job is to tackle the player with the ball

division—a small grouping of sports teams that often play one another; usually there are several divisions of teams in a conference.

interceptions—catches made by a defensive player of a pass thrown by the opposing team

linebacker—a player on defense whose main job is to make tackles and stop passes; a linebacker stands just behind the defensive linemen.

playoffs—the games played after the regular NFL season is over; playoff games determine which teams play in the Super Bowl.

punter—a player whose job is to dropkick the ball to the opposing team

quarterback—a player on offense whose main job is to throw and hand off the ball

rivals—teams that are long-standing opponents

running back—a player on offense whose main job is to run with the ball

sacked—tackled for a loss of yards; defenders can sack quarterbacks.

safety—a player on defense whose main job is to prevent wide receivers from catching the ball; a safety is positioned behind all the other players on defense.

solar panels—flat panels that use the sun's light or heat to create power

Super Bowl—the championship game for the NFL

tight end—a player on offense whose main jobs are to catch the ball and block for teammates

wind turbines—tall structures with large, fanlike blades that turn wind energy into electricity

TO LEARN MORE

AT THE LIBRARY

Frisch, Nate. *The Story of the Philadelphia Eagles*. Mankato, Minn.: Creative Education, 2014.

Stewart, Mark. *The Philadelphia Eagles*. Chicago, Ill.: Norwood House Press, 2013.

Wyner, Zach. *Philadelphia Eagles*. New York, N.Y.: AV2 by Weigl, 2015.

ON THE WEB

Learning more about the Philadelphia Eagles is as easy as 1, 2, 3.

1. Go to www.factsurfer.com.

2. Enter "Philadelphia Eagles" into the search box.

3. Click the "Surf" button and you will see a list of related web sites.

With factsurfer.com, finding more information is just a click away.

INDEX

The images in this book are reproduced through the courtesy of: Winslow Townson/ AP Images, front cover (large); Corbis, front cover (small), pp. 4-5, 7, 16, 16-17, 20-21, 23 (right), 28; Tony Gutierrez/ AP Images, p. 5; Larry W. Smith/ EPA/ Newscom, pp. 6-7; Joe Rimkus Jr./ KRT/ Newscom, pp. 8-9; Cal Sport Media/ Alamy, pp. 10-11; Ffooter, p. 11 (top); Justin Lane/ EPA/ Newscom, p. 11 (bottom); Brad Penner/ USA Today Sports/ Newscom, pp. 12-13; Deposit Photos/ Glow Images, pp. 12-13 (logos), 18-19 (logos), 28-29 (logos); Anthony Camerano/ AP Images, p. 14 (left); Pro Football Hall of Fame/ AP Images, p. 14 (right); Nate Fine/ Getty Images, p. 15; AP Images, p. 18 (top); Harold P. Matosian/ AP Images, p. 18 (bottom); Vernon Biever/ AP Images, p. 19 (top left); Jerry Lodriguss/ KRT/ Newscom, p. 19 (top right); NFL Photos/ AP Images, p. 19 (bottom left); Sportswire/ AP Images, p. 19 (bottom right); Rob Tringali/ SportsChrome/ Newscom, p. 21; Eric Mencher/ KRT/ Newscom, pp. 22-23; David Durochik/ AP Images, p. 22 (left); Focus On Sport/ Getty Images, p. 22 (middle); Al Messerschmidt/ AP Images, p. 22 (right); David Madison/ Getty Images, p. 23 (left); John Pyle/ Cal Sport Media/ Newscom, p. 23 (middle); Scott Anderson, p. 24; Tribune Content Agency LLC/ Alamy, p. 25; Vinny Carchietta/ ZUMA Press/ Newscom, p. 26; Brian Garfinkel/ AP Images, pp. 26-27, 29 (mascot); Tupungato, p. 29 (stadium).